Copper Carnation

A Collection of Poetry

RADOMIR VOJTECH LUZA

authorHOUSE

AuthorHouse™
1663 Liberty Drive
Bloomington, IN 47403
www.authorhouse.com
Phone: 833-262-8899

Published by AuthorHouse 06/02/2021

ISBN: 978-1-6655-2768-2 (sc)
ISBN: 978-1-6655-2769-9 (e)

Library of Congress Control Number: 2021911045

Print information available on the last page.

Contents

Introduction

This is Radomir Vojtech Luza's 33rd book (29th collection of poetry).

This is his brave and beautiful incarnation COPPER CARNATION.

Poem by poem, with precious few words, Luza's amplitude is felt. His depth and breadth of life is experienced. His creative brilliance startles.

He writes with a passion and a poignancy of the sweet and of the bitter. At times it seems like insurmountable juggernauts plague Luza's general well-being. In"Resurrected" I do not hang on the cross/But bang on the box/Of patience and pause. In "Bain Drain" The powerfully evocative stanza: Please do not talk to me of depression or mental illness/But of a broken heart burning out/Like a matchstick in a lagoon. And in "Lymphedema Lost" Luza's confidence is shaken: Staring at swollen gams/Like growing yams. His vulnerability and pain sear the page.

But a sparkling bouquet of lovelights, four or more Patricia poems appear. Luza's beloved shining being, his fiancee Patricia. In the poem "Patricia" little rare jeweled stanzas: The knees on you caress/Like rivers. You kiss/By not kissing Like a fawn you run/Like a heroin addict you shoot/Like a lover you leap. In the poem "Sunlight Through An Open Door (For Patricia)" Stretching sin into storage bin/Like sunshine through a sewing pin. Luza's child eye freshness amazes.

There are many marvels to behold in this book you hold. And last, but not least of the 78, comes the "Spring Slasher."

The slasher comes with mid-afternoon showers and plays by his own rules. And with him come the brutality and pathos of The slasher does anything/But scour The petals separating from the very/Stem of the flowers And later, Luza's indestructible image of a charming and alarming slasher: Has no conscience/Peppermint pink boots/Sun yellow apron Smelling like carnations in the garden/Daisies in the field His fame preceding him/Like Elvis Presley's pelvis

--Sigrid Bergie Feliciano--04/24/21

Dedication

I dedicate this book, then, my 33rd (29th collection of Poetry), to an Angel named Patricia, namely Patricia Murphy. This rainbow unicorn has been as loving, compassionate and empathetic a fiancé as one could hope for.

Not only has the blonde beauty conducted her own Stress Train over the last year-and-a-half as my Lymphedema and ability to walk have deteriorated, her condominium in Santa Clarita required a cruise ship full of blood, sweat and tears to fix up and she had to embrace the little things I used to do like paying the bills, getting gas for and taking care of our car, but this Nectar of Neon had to deal with loneliness and true doubt for the first time in a Decade.

This Crimson Fairy has so far visited me a dozen times or more in my nursing home in a little over two weeks and has been the only visitor since Visitation resumed.

Words do not describe the debt I owe this Galloping Gazelle nor the admiration and respect I have for her.

I thank God every waking moment that he made her mine to have and hold forever and a day.

I consider myself deeply blessed and the luckiest man on the face of this Daquiri Asteroid to get to call her potent and pure name my own.

Patricia, my robust realist, has been through the Meat Grinder and come-out more Fragrant than a Carnation.

I pray it always remains that way.

This book, then, is also dedicated to the Los Angeles Poetry Community which motivates me when I need it, nudges me creatively when I am down and uninspired and has truly been part of an outpouring of love through my GO FUND ME Campaign. I could not have made it without you.

The past 18 months have been incredibly difficult for me, but knowing that you poets are there one way or another truly makes all the difference in the world.

May each and every one of you stay healthy, wise and never give-up on yourself, your imagination or your potential.

God bless you All, Now and Forever!!!!

--RADOMIR VOJTECH LUZA--4/10/21

Prior Publications

THE HARAHAN JOURNAL – Collection of Poetry
Dinstuhl Publishing (New Orleans)

THIS N' THAT – Collection of Prose
Dinstuhl

PORCH LIGHT BLUES – Collection of Poetry
BT Publishing (Oakland, CA) Beverly Tilghman

BROKEN HEADLIGHTS – Collection of Poetry
Pigling Bland Press (Langhorne, PA)

AIRPORTS AND RAILROADS – Collection of Prose
Pigling Bland

TACKS AND ROOT BEER – Short Collection of Prose and Poetry
Ron Swegman Publishing (Philadelphia, PA)

A PRAYER FOR MONICA – Collection of Love Poetry
Pigling Bland

SHOES IN A MAGAZINE – Collection of Older Poetry
Pigling Bland

DIVA DANDRUFF – Personal Essays
Author House (Bloomington, IN)

BLUE SKY SCHOOL – Collection of Children's Poetry
Author House

SCOLIOSIS OF RAIN – Collection of Poetry
Author House

48 ON THE FLOOR – Self-Published Manuscript of 48 Poems
(Jersey City, NJ)

EVERYTHING BUT…-Self-Published Manuscript of Prose
(Jersey City, NJ)

STAGE SCRIBBLINGS – Collection of Theatre Reviews
Aurorean Music Weekly (Northern and Central NJ and NYC) (Jersey City, NJ)

STARVING SWALLOWS – Collection of Poetry
Publish America (Baltimore, MD)

TO THE NINES – Poetry Collection (Luza and Don Kingfisher Campbell)
Campbell published it through his small press (Alhambra, CA)

DAMAGED GOODS – Collection of Poetry
Dancing Sprite Publications (Radman Productions) (North Hollywood, CA)

PERSONAL POEMS – Collection of Family Poems
Poets on Site (Pasadena, CA)

MORE PERSONAL POEMS – Collection of Family Poems
Poets on Site

THE LAST COLLECTION – Collection of Poetry
Publish America

THE FOURTH NUTHOUSE IN SEPTEMBER – Collection of Short Poetry
Publish America

ROPE: Two poems
Marymark Press

CAFÉ LATTE TAPES – Collection of poetry
Publish America

NEW YORK NADIR – Collection of Poetry
Author House

EROS OF ANGELS – Collection of Poetry and Prose
Author House

WINDY CITY SONGS – Collection of Poetry
Red Doubloon Publishing (Radman Productions)

TALE OF TWO TOWNS – Collection of Poetry
Red Doubloon

CLIFFS, CALM AND COYOTES – Collection of Poetry
Red Doubloon

SIDEWALKS AND STREET CORNERS-Collection of Poetry
Christian Faith Publishing
(Meadville, PA)

MENTAL MALL-A Collection of Poetry
Four Feathers Press
(Pasadena, CA)

ONYX ROSE
Christian Faith Publishing

About the Author

Radomir Vojtech Luza is a longtime poet whose sensitivity and talent have triumphed over a bipolar mental illness, homelessness and Lymphedema which he contracted in 2016 and that attacks the lymph nodes and prevents a person from walking normally due to swelling.

Writing Verse has been a welcome escape since 1986. It takes the veteran SAG/AFTRA/AEA Union Actor and Stand-Up Comedian, improvisational performer, host and Theatre, Film and Book Critic (www.atthetheatrewithRadomirLuza.com) to Pinker Pastures and Magenta Meadows.

The Tulane University and Jesuit High School (New Orleans, LA) Graduate was born in Vienna, Austria in 1963 and gets his love of art and politics from his renowned Czech parents.

The Poet Laureate of North Hollywood, CA since 2012 is also a Pushcart Prize Nominee (2012) and the Author of 33 books (29 collections of Poetry) since 1991, the last two: MENTAL MALL, a 20-Poem Chapbook from Four Feathers Press in Pasadena, CA that was published in 2020 and ONYX ROSE, the 200+page Collection of Poetry and Prose that will be Published later this year by Christian Faith Publishing in Meadville, PA.

The 2021 San Gabriel Valley Poetry Festival Book Contest First-Place Winner for LOSING ME: POEMS FROM BED 23C and Broadside Poem Contest Finalist won Third Place in The New Orleans' Catholic Youth Organization's Man of the Year Contest in 1983. The First CYO Member from St. Rita Church in Harahan, LA Ever to Place.

The Irwin Award Winner (Book Publicists of Southern California) for "Most Creative Collection of Poetry" for EROS OF ANGELS, his 400-page Magnum Opus (2016), has had his Verse Published in over 80 literary journals, anthologies and websites such as Askew, Poetry Motel, Poet, Papyrus (Cover), Lummox, Journal of Modern Poetry, Los Angeles Daily News, Bent Pin Quarterly, Writers of the Desert Sage, Pegasus, Spare Change, KYSO Flash, Spectrum, Altadena Poetry Review,

Altadena Literary Review, Bicycle Review, Cultural Weekly, Poetrysuperhighway.com, Boog City, Boston Globe, The Eintouist, Writers Digest, Highlandparkpoetry.org, Sahara, New Laurel Review, Roguescholars.com, Lucidmoonpoetry.com, Sage Trail, Men in the Company of Women and Skysage, among others.

The Fiction and Creative Non-Fiction Writer and former President of the North Hollywood West Neighborhood Council (Los Angeles, CA) (2013-17), Member of the North Hollywood NC (2010-17) and former Democratic Candidate for Auditor in Middletown Township, Bucks County outside Philadelphia, PA has had his Written Word Featured over 100 times across the Country.

The Catholic of nearly 50 years has also Organized, Curated and Hosted over 15 Poetry Reading Series across the nation in places such as Jersey City, NJ, Hoboken, NJ, New York, NY, Fort Walton Beach, FLA and Los Angeles, CA.

The BA in English and Graduate of Holy Name of Jesus Elementary School (New Orleans, LA), has co-organized and is the primary host of the UNBUCKLED: No Ho POETRY series with Mary Aneetta Mann for over ten years at T.U. Studios in North Hollywood, CA.

The Editor and Publisher of the Literary Magazine, VOICES IN THE LIBRARY, Published by Red Doubloon Press, the Literary Arm of Radman Productions, allows his Poetic Soul to Lead him up the Literary Bridge to God which he considers to be Poetry.

--RADOMIR VOJTECH LUZA--4/11/21

Sherbet Shark

Pink and blue like Rumpelstiltskin stew
Rainbow ring around horizon's king

Sing, oh, sing you sunrise bling
Edelweiss clouds reaching
Children staring
Few caring

Unicorns rushing in
Fairies brushing off last sin

Dawn over trees and bushes
Still as arrested lushes

Orange pewter yellow as frozen butter

Sylvia Plath in my hair
Pablo Neruda my stare
Robert Frost my holy unholy glare

Drowning in blood-soaked air
Laughing at departing moon

Who am I?
Where am I going?
Does my future have a June?

Peppermint sky never a lie
Fading ink like weak drink

Cherubic smile at 5:43 a.m.
I exhale
Medication no longer stale

Tomorrow clear as day
Yesterday red as clay

Today oblong
Cobalt new
Not red as pink zoo

Suffocating in bubble gum air
Off-magenta lair

Morning

Breath as large as Brando when he died
Arms thicker than the Mississippi River
Legs potent as moonbeams

Maybe the time between take-off and landing
Will straighten out the gullies and glades

Oh, morn
Feeding children to the blue sky
Parents the electric high

Take, oh, take the sun away
And let it bake

Like a spider
For God's sake

Your bronze eyes
Wheat skin

Face of a fairy
Black the berry

Skirmish in the woods
Burning the nascent goods

Dawn take me as your victim times three
The very American red, white and blue flavor to inspire tea

Telling me of some far away threat
They all forget my running bet

That resilience and rapture always go further
Than brilliance and capture

In morning's mouth
Turning South for a change

Car Lights

In bated breath
Invaded meth

I see your car lights
Shimmering under moon glow
Shining like star flow

Sharp as college professors
Large as owl eyes
Quick as gorilla cries

You are my car light
My reason for being
My artist's way of seeing

The river of you decadent and dark
Now neon and electric
Like strapping eel

I was
I am
I will be

Car lights at the border
Car lights striking down the slaughter

Car lights coming from the soul like hot coal
Car lights drowning in black like heart attack

Car lights fueled by love
Like lonesome dove above

Car lights shredding indifference like
Atom bombs of deliverance

Gentle Rain

Like rose petals falling
Tender snowflakes calling

Have I allowed myself to be touched?
Ever caressed?
Even taken by someone other than myself?

Let the gentle rain fall
Like bubbles bursting in two

Ladles of spring water
Spreading my lips so blue
My retinas so true

In puddles of rain
Ponds of same
Streams to blame

I am now around you
Your twinkling turquoise two
The rainbow-colored kaleidoscope pair

Unicorn duo on the prowl
Raindrops falling on my shoulders
Like wet boulders
Coyote howling like train whistle in early morn

Gentle rain on my tresses like pain

Hair like wheat shorn
From skull torn
Born in worn corn like porn

Gentle rain, oh, gentle rain
Please do not come again

Mother earth will keep me sane

Seeking Silver

Tigers are late
Lions early
In a world of oats and wild goats

I often wonder where we would be
If God made us free

Under an oak tree or willow
Without a seed perhaps

But my questions have no answers
For God is a spirit
In search of a mountain

Girls like dolls
Boys small cars

Women bras
Men sports cars

So where is it written that this royal blue orb
Will rotate forever

For there is no road map of the wilderness
No guide to nature

Only you and me
And the need to be

Still as the Indian Ocean
Rough as the Black Sea

Sprinting towards happiness
Galloping to nirvana
Leaping and lunging toward a larger affinity

Smoking the sky
With a weathered cry

I have learned
Not to ask why

Patricia On Key

Hair like shorn wheat
Lips red meat
Hips swivel seat

Laughing through saltwater
Weeping at emotional slaughter

I swear you are the most beautiful thing
I have ever seen

I live to touch your rose petal skin
Without original sin

Kissing the forehead
As a prom pin

Tender luscious you are
Legs like mannequin models

Breath like stardust powder
Arms like soft down
Eyes a bitter crown
Ears two nimble frowns

Speaking that oft unfiltered mind

Tapping unstilted grind
Unsettled kind

Child of the sun
Electric as the one

Neon like fun
Radiant as a gun

Driving me to the scrum
Like mother
You beat your own drum

I would walk around the world
To take one look at you my little girl

Sunlight Through An Open Door

(For Patricia)

Stretching sin into storage bin
Like sunshine through a sewing pin

Ray of light
Like spray of sight

Flowing through hole in space
Without a can of mace

Jam, jam the door with
Anything but night

On this mid-afternoon flight
Of fancy and might

Shine, sparkle, shimmer
Through a straight line

Jackhammering mine
Like red wine

On a ripe day when you clutch the month of May

I Will Always Love You

No matter the darkness I may wander
The jungles that do not see me through
Car accidents drawing my last breath
I will always love you

Through all the lions' manes and tiger's tales
The concentration camps of despair and humiliation
The very guns I display hoping they will be taken away

Over mountains and plains
Fields and rains

Below peaks and cliffs
Above valleys and rifts

I will climb to you
Through tangled oceans
Poisoned potions

Diabolical motions
Depressed notions
I will always love you

No matter the pawns I take
Queens I break

Time I take
Existence I rake
Stupidity I bake
I will always love you

For love is God
You the Master's daughter

Role

The part I play in this inverted game
This silly, silly same
Is not of a noble name

But a unique and rare flame
Circling the estuaries and lakes

For any sign of blame I revel in
Portraying my character
On stage and screen

To an audience lean and keen
About every scene

Giving a turn of such finesse
And rhythm
Sanity and spice

That even the most gifted playwright
Would stop eating rice

For the mask I don not knowing
Whether I will return

Yet stowing my luggage so far
Inside my soul I will never
Gain control of this totem pole

Built like ceramic bowl
Because even it has a hole

Stole

You took from me all that was good
The only part of me that was free
That lived on an island of coffee and tea

You burglarized my soul for the penny that you stole
Molested my brain again and again
For the blackness that you stained

Trudged on the very grass of my heart
The one you darkened without so much
As a name

The goal you managed without an ounce of game
Grabbing the day you abruptly ended
My lengthy stay
Away, away

By bludgeoning the beast inside
The wondering, wandering tiger of my tail
Once more flirting with every extreme

You cut open my inseam of love
Like a midnight dove with wings
Never reaching above

Misguided and misjudged I look to the horizon
Daquiri green and strawberry banana

But even that does not add up to a stolen moment
Obliterated from view by the
Plane crash that was you

Hole

In the abstract ether of this universe
My hole barely matters
Hardly counts for anything but depth and duty

The wicked opening is the warlock's wounded wagon
Beelzebub's broken bannister of bacon
The gargoyle's boulevard of blitzed brain
Desperate drain

I fell in like fluid water
A loud quarter

Only to find the other side
Transparent skin of me
Translucent sin of three

Dark and dank as broken soil
Wide and long as this orphaned boil

Blood and sweat as I toil
Against the darkness in my soul

The very clit of this hole
By and by ask me not about
My bleakness

By the weakness of my purpose
The obliqueness of the heart and sky

Neither connected by more than name
But part of the same game
This well's naked blame

Mole

In the mix of pores and pain
Skin and rain

The children matter in the
Finished batter

For they at least know the face of slaughter
The unwelcome caterwauling
Of awkward laughter

At this intersection of
Snow and brain
Flow and grain

Lies the solution
To time's refrain

How we exist and
How it hardly matters

Leaping from atom to molecule
With all the swiftness of a rented mule

The abscess on your nose
Candid echo of your pose

Leaves but torn memories
Burnt sentries

In the annals of man
I will not find another with a

Temper so short or
Distemper so long

As to destroy today's horizon
Without a song

Land a spear in the stained glass windows
Of my fears

Like a rapist consoling his victims
For the good of his peers

Laguna at Dusk

Dodger blue sky and indenting swan white lie
Southern California dash and flash
Finding orange sun in 1981

Cement and stucco buildings
Reflecting electric light

Cobalt blue water shimmering upwards
Like scorned girlfriend

Hands held
Feet furiously forward
Beaches abandoned

Romeo eatery on Broadway welcoming
Another weekday evening crowd

Yes meaning no
No meaning yes
Both a salty mess
At 5:39 P.M. horizon narrowing like
Jeans in the 1970's

Waiting for my lady love, Patricia
Penning poetry at the shore

A sensitivity like hers
Uncommon and rare

In a town where attraction and
Confusion go hand-in-hand

Like red brake lights and royal blue sky
Licorice sticks and rhubarb pie
Do not ask why

On this third Wednesday in February
Winter feels shorn and worn like
An old mink coat

Spring a skip and jump away
Like a day in May
On this Orange County hamlet of
Neon ray and rusty gray

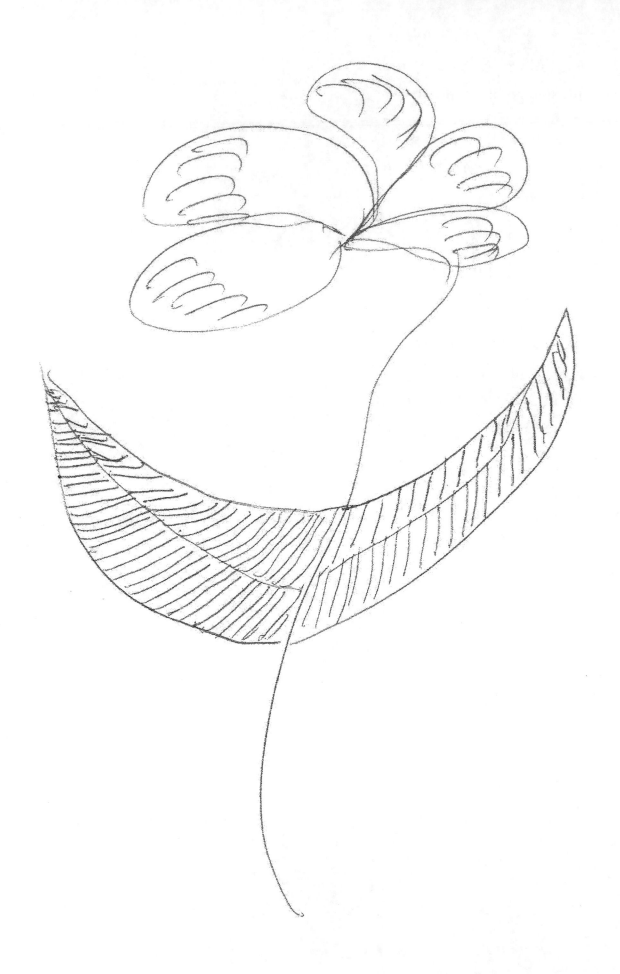

Writing on Her Mask

Ocean North of my soul
Abducted by a wounded hole
Soiled by the sordid sea
Does she ever think about me?

Sailboat traversing hidden lake
She never stops playing with
Poisonous snakes
Hours of shrapnel in my head
From the bullets she launched in lead
A living room of misery born instead

Cheering on her demise in red
My voice gone and she is still not dead
Take my heart before it ceases to start

Building castles that look like walls
Forts that are modern malls

Eyes of you like brown potatoes
Growing in boxes like frozen oxes

Maybe just this once you will think of
Someone else

Before diving off that
Black and bloodied beach

Fiancé of Flowers

Taking those scattered waves
Making tattered saves

Where rhyming is left home
Metaphors are only for the needy

Assonance the greedy
Alliteration the seedy

Thread of time thickening with you by my side
The very yarn of life not receding

Color me orange like your eyes when they laugh
Transparent as glacier lakes when they weep

My dearest Patricia
I lick your high arching cheekbones

Kiss those chocolate red lips
As you swing your beautifully curved hips

On this continent of stale contracts and heavy whips
Flushing the blood from your veins never more difficult

When dancing to nothing at the shore
Opening something near the door
Falling to slumber on the floor

Patricia, you red-hooded lioness
Braving and saving my dreams

As naked and raw
As Elvis Presley's seams and schemes

Thunderstorms like Long, Deep Tunnels

Precipitation from the sky
By and by
Spraying trees, tomahawks and tepid tundra

Rain showers like Satan's army
George Patton's tank brigade
At midnight falling non-stop

Biting soil, sand and stone
Like water on bone
Sheets of pain wear
Heat of insane

Lightning leaping and lunging in sky
Like tormented, twisted and
Torn tin man

Thunder rumbling like God stumbling
In this meadow of branches and
Horseless ranches

Hail polluting oxygen like
Baseballs at spring training

I am truer than horizon's light
Our sacred fight

Dancing in destiny's night
This hologram of unseen sight

Porcelain Plague

Caressing this pandemic with gentle hands
On tender lands
Like a yearling's glands

Never attacking it
Taking it apart or ransacking its living room or
Torpedoing its cellar

Instead behaving like invited guests
Saying hello and thank you when instructed

Sipping from the correct wine glass
When asked
Eating from the proper side

Where is our purpose
Our mission
Why are we not more aggressive

We should blitzkrieg the virus
And ask questions later

Instead we are kind and polite
And now hang corpses wrapped in body bags
Out of refrigerated trucks in Times Square

The boulevard to death is jackhammered
By roses and rouge

Thrashed

Four mental hospitals
Bipolar diagnosis
Homelessness in city
I do not know

Near deadly divorce
Mother dead of
Ovarian cancer at 72

Sister absent
For 15 years

Lymphedema and arthritis
Swollen legs and aching pegs
Hospitals and Nursing Home

I am beaten-up
But not bruised

Thrashed but
Not mashed

Seeing the blue
In your brown eyes

Hearing Spring
In your Winter

Feeling a poem
Burning your skin

The front lawn
Emblazoning your forehead

The pinkest of meadows
Tattooing the
Wettest of tongues

Metaphors mingling with
Mania to vomit words
Unspoken by yapping herds

Poetry keeping
My heart beating
My soul bleeding

God never dying
As we slumber
Restlessly trying

Mental Mall

Glass egg in center of rotund hall
Beige walls
Palpable pall

Doctors and nurses in vanilla coats
Dispensing light blue and pink
Oval-shaped pills in paper cups

Self-conscious sojourns
Into narrow, neutral stalls
Smelling like Bedford Falls

Talking to medicated patients in
Salt white gowns
With trembling hands
Shaking thighs
No purpose or passion to fly

Shrinks playing ping pong
In middle of floor
Ignoring front and back door
Patients without a sore

I am nothing
No one
All meaning has been lost
Hope abandoned
Love barricaded

Friends afraid to come
Parents missing some
Sister losing sorority cred with each med

Sleeping with six men in one room
Death looming
Mental paralysis fuming

Body aching
Brain disjointed
Subconscious disoriented
Bipolar diagnosis

Where is my Joe DiMaggio?

I went three times
I went four
I want no more

Flowers with No Sages

On days that are long
Composing elegies of rock and stone

On days that are short
Waves drowning the shore like elegant whores

Disaster after depression
Diving before dining

Life unbearable without people
Praying in steeple

With no one to stroke
Visages fashioned in hell

But children torn from cages
Born of Beelzebub's ages

During hours that are strong
Time is long

In the minutes that follow
Seconds soaring like bionic sparrow

Bullets into infant's beak
Moments made of lead sinking deep

Pleas of sweetened meat
Scattered at your feet

This parade careening down Main
And onto Maple

Does not stop
Cannot pop and drop

Winding its way through your gums
Like milk and wine

Flowing like lazy river
Without rhyme

Downtown

Where the protestors sang
Looters ran
Police had no plan

Where it all began
To a man
Exploded like a fan

Downtown
Downtown

Children never come
Darkness a constant hum
Stench of bitter rum

Blaring and sharing
The city's nouveau riche
Like Vikings stranded on a beach

Downtown
Downtown

This Central Business District
Second to none
In non-clarification and
A setting sun

Where demonstrators stood
With a smoking gun
And nowhere to run

City Hall taking it on the chin
Like a big brother loaded with sin
Forgetting duty for a fake grin

Downtown
Downtown

This revolution is televised
Down where the blue review
Cameras and reporters like an electric zoo

Marking the spot where barricades and cruisers
Fell into hell
Beneath a heinous smell

Quivering hands
Ringing golden bell

I Cannot Fight What I Feel

(Dedicated to Fred LeBlanc of the
Band Cowboy Mouth)

Whenever I get around you
Even if I'm a thousand miles away

Tears flow
Hearts glow
My soul takes a blow

I wish I could stop
But I love you

Through trembling calves and
Shaking wrists
Scars healing and emotions peeling

I feel you everywhere I go
From my nose to my toes

The admiration and respect second to none

For you have done it
Hook, line and blinker

While I have but dreamed it
Brook, mine and tinker

Your present choking the past from me
Like an absolute beginner

Patricia

Your hands like scissors
Cut through the ribbons of my intestines

I hold the air around your face
Like a carbon copy of time

The knees on your caress
Like rivers

I would spend dollars on you
If I could

But you are more than money
More than mountains
More than stolen sunsets

You kiss
By not kissing

Like a fawn you run
Like a heroin addict you shoot
Like a lover you leap

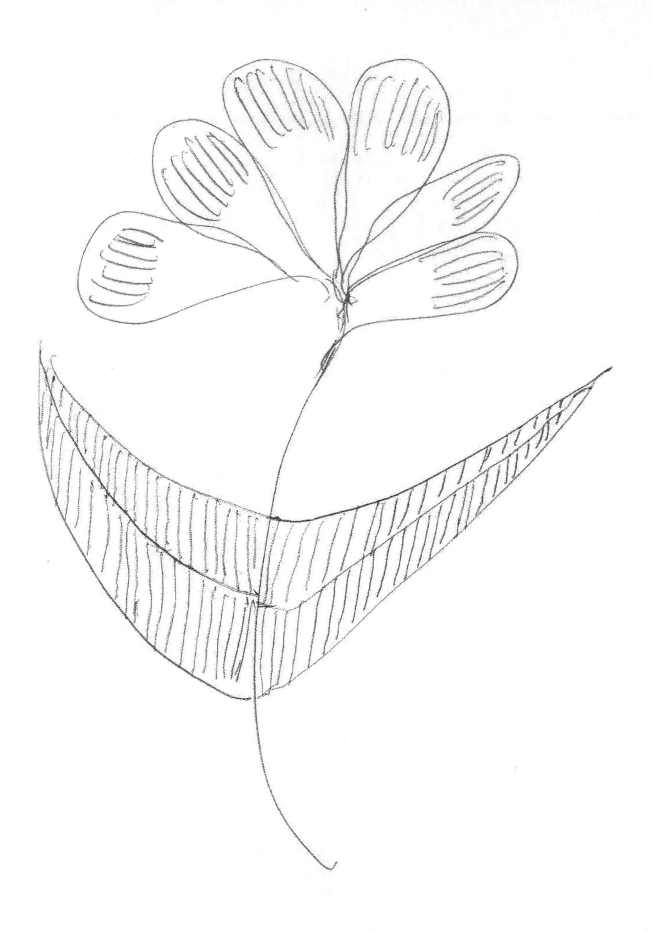

Mug of Dawn

Peach clouds
Across Daiquiri sky
I don't ask why

Above palm trees and
Rush hour traffic

God must have created earth
In seven days

This planet
A reflection of his face

Every dimple and
High cheekbone
Pimple and broken nose

Birds flying across
Tangerine horizon

Mountains in the distance
Like dark green elephants
Underneath sherbet roof

The rhubarb eyes
Spinach ears of him

Visible in every inch of
Neo-alabaster ceiling

November has
Beautiful teeth

Shaping Your Face Like a Green Garden

Grass in the middle
Rocks to the right
Soil on my left

Sunshine bursting through like love
My tongue high as an alabaster dove

Pain narrowing
Suffering descending
Cellar stairs like angry black bear

Feeling your face with my hands
Like misplaced grace at the battle of the bands

Digging and diving
Ditching and thriving

Your countenance lovelier than a Summer's bray
More beautiful than Winter's white blanket day

Autumn's smorgasbord of orange and brown
Spring's festival of solace and down

Lingering Latitude

When sunset sings
Like a lark's last swing

Dusk crawls to the edge
Of the tender hook

Like worn book
Master crook

Blue streaking across pink ribbons of sky
Your mother's hazel eyes in my cry

Stew of berries and brew
Like skin of sin
Bargaining beneath stolen sun's torn tantrums

Night closes the door
Darkness even more
On this open store

Light fading like love degrading
Perhaps it is God I see at 7:53

Pandemic Party

Whether piano or air guitar
Music is flooding the pandemic
Like a pregnant hurricane

The sole trumpeteer in the
French Quarter in New Orleans

The citizens of New York and Italy
Applauding and banging pots every night
To celebrate health care workers

Anyone and everyone using their
Spare Covid-19 time to learn or
Re-learn an instrument

Whether the breeze
A sneeze or
Cracking knees

Music glues itself to the soul
Tapes itself to the heart
Covers the wounded brain

Offering solace, tranquility and peace
God's guitar
St. Peter's drum snare
Will leave your being bare

Or ram a hole through the pandemic's
Glare

With harps, violins and flares
Music soars into Corona's stare
And burns its hair down to there

It almost seems unfair

Malignant Marble

Trapped in a world of
Crimson balloons
Exploding lakes

Freeways and byways crisscrossing
The volcanoes and tsunamis of your eyes

The very unfurling monsters
In your bed

This blue asteroid shifting and shaking
Billowing and baking

Like a lost linebacker running at
Invisible dummies

Or a President listening to
Jaded tongues

Caged in a bubble
Of our own making

Whispers and walruses
At the ready

Boulders and belfries
Going steady

Turquoise stones
Bipolar bones

Living to die
Dying to live

Eating to survive
Worms of cold

In a golden orb
Never bold

Children marching
On temerity and time

Tell them
Oh, tell them
That God is blind

Early Evening Mid-Autumn Los Angeles Laundromat Blues

I park in a handicapped spot for the first time ever about 6:45 PM on this Tuesday
in early November
Few people here speak English
Even less own washers and dryers
Fewer yet say hello back when I say it to them

I sometimes think of the laundromats in the videos on Pornhub.com
Where dignity, integrity and detergent take a back seat to lust, incest and adultery

This huge scrub hub on Magnolia Boulevard in North Hollywood, CA
Stays open from 6 AM to 2 AM and has no name

I often wonder how it has managed to survive for so long
Given its often small amount of customers
It reminds of Death Valley on a Monday in the Winter

I sit in my ulcer red 2012 Toyota Prius and
Let my fiancé Patricia do the washing and drying due to my Lymphedema

I feel like an outsider looking in
A burden to friends and family
Sometimes I ponder suicide

Inside people look at me in my brand new
NBA green and white Giannis Antetokounmpo
Milwaukee Bucks jersey while they fold clothes

I remind myself that I am more than the clothes I wear
I am God's child
I seek truth wherever it may be

As my mother always told me
If you are good at something
You never stop being good at it

I am a talented poet, actor and comedian
With a galaxy of patience

Around 8 PM we leave the polyester palace
Soon food trucks and customers will surround
My favorite washing well

For us there is no looking back
Only staring straight ahead

Six Million Feet High

Delta flight 403
London to Vienna

Row 13 seats A and B
Mother and me

Seat C
Austrian man
Telling mother that
Holocaust did not happen

"Es war nicht," he says in German

Czech mother
War survivor

Stands up and blurts out
Her best German

"Es war und es war sehr schlecht"

The slaughter took place and
Was very bad, she says

Finally free
Without apathy
Mother sits down
In B

I stop shaking knee
Order hot tea

Empty Sky

There are days
When this world
Is insane

Losing its mooring
From reason
Tethered to the moon

Floating like a balloon
Towards the sun

Nothing makes sense
No one can explain anything

Love has been lost
Balance stolen

Logic unfurled
Like a flag
In a hurricane

We are witches in a
Cauldron of doubt

Warlocks seeking trembling wrists and
Knocking knees
Before steady palms and straight legs

Thinking only of ourselves we
Perish like mice
Settle like dust

This planet is a frightening orb
Road-weary asteroid

Falling when rising
Breaking when bending

In corners and crevices
Deals are made with the devil

Snakes slithering
Towards the exits

While this crazy blue marble
Explains itself in hues of
Magenta and gold

Boulevards are sold
Tragedy foretold

Camouflage

Beneath the golden mermaids
Flippers of bronze

Lie oceans
Made of wood

Rivers flowing backwards
Skies bending upwards

For in this
Divided nation

Politicians are
Losing their minds

Children do not
Know their parents

Priests are
Releasing their faith

Parents their
Trust in each other

We are living in an
Omelette made of camouflage

A whirling, twirling
Rubber ball of doubt

A Pepsi Cola blue
Asteroid of Cancer and death

Is there
No way out?

No mourning
For the forsaken?

No straight line
Instead of extremes?

Pieces of Myself

(Written at the laundromat across from Ralph's on
Magnolia Boulevard, North Hollywood, CA)

I am finding pieces of myself
Parts I left behind or never did really find
Anger and tons of fear
Stomping out magenta butterflies

Tall peacocks kicking off my socks
Doubt and King Lear
Blocking love
Taping off heaven above

Early morning dove flying into jungle snare
Locating moments of indefinite glare
Sending off flair for remaining pieces
In midair

Where have I gone?
Who am I?

Does public opinion matter?
Where am I going?

Sometimes the path begs for moon glowing
Sun stowing

Coming across who I was
Who I wanted to be
When jumping into the sea

Why at 57 I only feel prepared to take
Bold risks now
Sprinting like a galloping sow

Shining white light on sections of psyche
Never before seen pieces of me
Shards of three

Grandfather Grace

Through mud and weed
Rock and stone

Horizon still mattering
Dreams never shattering

Fire has a heart that does
Not need a switch to start

As our aspirations murder in overdrive
Wrists thin as Root Beer bottles

Dot the landscape of our bodies
Like arrogant boxers
Angry golfers
Aggressive linebackers

Roof of our mouths
Not touching tongue

On momentum preceding
Hand grenades fading
Centipedes waiting

I look for the ying and yang
In your eyes

But all I see are cardboard boxes
Raspberry foxes

The compromise of clouds
Balance of Bison

Learning to unlearn
Giving to take

Forgiving like snakes
On this marble of madness
Dish of darkness

Shepherd leading
Saints needing
Angels feeding

Your fare a beaded cornucopia
Of perfection squared

Solace In The Cellar

In the inglorious moments of life
I find the most purpose

In the unimportant chess pieces
Of our time
Lie the most significant minutes

In the catastrophic existences
We all lead
Live the most necessary people
Who know only how to lead
And never to follow

In the haunted hours of the
Early morning
All but the brave fall to their knees

As the river washes away
The good for the bad

Nervous wrists replacing steady hands
Knocking knees taking the place of
Rented legs

Imagination falling prey to knowledge
Art to commerce

It is the darkest of times
Blackest of rhymes

Bloated and beaten
I pray for enlightenment
And reincarnation

I receive a bullet in the head
A eulogy worth a month in bed

Black Sunday

On a hillside in Calabasas, CA
Kobe Bryant perished today
In a helicopter crash
Worse than anything on the
Television show MASH

With 13-year-old daughter Gianna in tow
God seemed to stoop low
On this last Sunday before the Super Bowl

Although he was highly imperfect
The Black Mamba possessed one of
The deadliest jump shots in
Professional basketball history

Often poisoning his opponent's
Chances at victory with one
Beautiful boulevard busting
Basket from the Staples Center
Parking lot

Black is the color today
Dark the sun ray

Kobe you will be missed
For you are by the angels and
Saints kissed

Like a celebrity athlete rocking the moon
Your month will forever be
Championship June

Eyes Like Red Apples

Your hands like pears
Soft and supple

Breasts like fresh peaches
Ripe and ample

I think of taking
You dwell on raking

But in the end
We do nothing

Which is much like
Doing something

We kiss and caress
Like old lovers or
Absolute beginners

Fresh lips
Curved hips
Skin like velvet
Cheekbones like satin
Golden blonde hair like wheat

Soul over sex
Heart above money

We trust mother earth
For she gave us birth

Creator

I sit and think
Spit and sink

I hardly read
Write like a flowing river

I am connected to the Master
Nature and everyone around me

I feed off that energy
Like a Boa Constrictor
A human head

Populate the notebook
With words

Pollute the horizon
With buffalo herds

Language of love
Up above
Like alabaster dove

Creating hurts
Like a bullet to the ribs
Lassoe around fingertips

It is not the imagination that matters
But what inspires it
The earth that gives it birth

Birth Mother

Poetry brought me here
Helped me find myself
Told me who I am

Poetry is my birth mother
Pregnant with pain
Full of the kind of cold
They only know in Maine

Cliffs and canyons
Glades and gullies
Meadows and marbles

Time sits the master
On mountain alabaster
Fending off disaster
Faster and faster

On the edge of her lips
I found the courage to write
Fight and discover light
At night

Perhaps she should not
Have had me

Only then would I have had to
Find another crack
To drown the lack

Before Breakfast

Strips of pink wrapping around
Cobalt sky

Clouds in cluster
Like General Custer

Trees like soldiers
Guarding the Queen
Maybe one day they
Will sway as they lean

Beach white as chalk
Water turquoise blue
Islands clad in aqua green

Birds quiet and mean
Part of this early morning scene

Bushes dollar green
Wiry as James Dean

Dawn disappearing
Dress shirt unbuttoning
Underwear unraveling

There, look, there
Pink is not red
But gray

Like dusk on a Sunday
Rust in mid-May

Chasing Shadows

Under the overpass
The homeless swig
Bottles of Jack Daniels
And Smirnov

In the bathroom stall
Teenage outsiders
Insert heroin into veins
Fly like rain
Before going insane

All I have I hold
Until time does fold

On the sets I build
With secret shastas filled

Once there was a chance at love
Now I stand on a mine
Where I do not walk the line

For what good is chance if
I do not dance

Why do I corral luck
For an extra buck?

Searching for my first tuck on
Boulevards and avenues
Of affiliated suck

Where corners are blood red
Crevices Dakota brown
Sidewalks Dracula dark

And the difference between
Breathing and dying is a healthy sound

When not busy chasing shadows
The monsters find me
Mannerisms in tow
Coming in low

I am history
Shining like the sun
Glowing like the moon

Never giving up on my dreams
Though ripped apart at the seams
Without schemes
Black hole teams

Blazing Rivers

Between power and pain
Live love and rain

One propelling the ark
The other singing in the dark

Under lazy freeways
Busy gamma rays
I dance dirges in the park

As jaded politicians jog in the wrong lane
I stand on mercy not gain

To alight onto a sturdier ledge
Where heroes and villains alike
Laugh with a new pledge

Beneath the bilge and banter
Of tattered troops and tarnished stoops

Blazing rivers
You will never understand

For only in wildest dreams
Hottest steams

Did you ever sacrifice for anything
Beyond the driest of creams

Suffocating on lost avenues
Bewildered boulevards

Tackling the extreme
By making a scene

Infusing the negative
By belating the positive

On these streams and fair
Tributaries were you not born

Only brought to pray
When evil scrapes your skin
Like a rash and jealousy
Your retina like a gash

Resurrected

The black has turned electric yellow
The dark a neon fellow

Sky burning magenta red
Learning where to tread
Without chains of lead

If only I had more grace

Tributaries and rivers would run to
The end of my face

Laughing and chortling Satan's song
Busted and brazen
My spiritual rap sheet is long

So, I am resurrected
From the old to the new
Many to the few

I do not hang on the cross
But bang on the box
Of patience and pause

Like a gun slinger
My hands are cheetah quick

My mind
Winston Churchill sharp

Go home, you Hollywood halos
Friends for a second of math

I banish you from the bedroom of my wrath

I am resurrected into the tranquil
Born again into the strong
Ascending into the thankful

Never forgetting my shell
Dragging myself from hell
Ringing the brand new bell

Silent Solstice

The golden bridge of my imagination
Leading to fame and riches
That in the end hardly matter

The red cloud integrity of my soul
The very iron clad dignity of my heart
Beats stronger than any art

Opening my eyes to the weeping of children
Their bellies
Uncaressed faces

The little voice in my gut flies to
Bethlehem and beyond

Opening my ears to their screaming
The very gnawing at the gates of Eden

The voices of irate synthesis
Puncturing victory laps

And I wonder at my childhood
Its spectre and spectacle

How it made little sense in a
World of gilded stares
Hurtful snares

Superficial lairs
Materialistic glares

My adulthood with its 35 years of
Suffering and silent sabotage

Scribbling poetic thunderbolts
Verse vacations

While this alabaster marble
Wakes and walks

To the saxophones and synthesizers
Of science and seminaries

Both lost in worlds of
Unagitated murder made clear by

Snickering fools and
Second-guessed rules

Father's Czech Accent

It lit up a room
With its sophisticated tongue
Refined nuance

Like an angel without a broom
Or a velvet sash on a satin robe

It had its own area and zip codes
The way it tore through the
English language
With tenderness and grace

A liquid face
Scientific base

An emerging politician
In his Czech homeland

Father did not consider
The challenge in America
Because of the accent

And, oh, what a mistake he made

The radiant smile
Worldly charm
Avid innocence
Painfully-earned wisdom

Could have made him a
Possible contender for the
Democratic Presidential Nomination

Though he would tell me to
Shut up if he heard me say it

His humility unable to grasp
A crown that heavy

A mission that fraught with
Fear and doubt

I wish father would have
Donned the contender's gloves

It would have changed his life
For the better

And mine for the best
It seems

Holy Hands

In tunnels and funnels
Parks like Larks

Now is the time to pass the rhyme
With the help of our holy hands

Whether painting like Picasso
Writing like Hemingway
Or painting pictures made of poetry
Like Arthur Rimbaud

Satan begs us to lose our minds
During this lockdown

Unholy war against an unseen opponent
Battle for a beloved balance

Use the creativity God gave you
The imagination of John Lennon
Passion of Sylvia Plath

And soar like a falcon to the sea
Using flowery fingers
Blessed thumbs to while away the time

Learn an instrument
Write an opera
Beckon the soul

Hearken to the heart
Make love before you start
Be another Beethoven or Mozart
Pen a symphony at Kmart

Be one more Shakespeare or Tennessee Williams
And populate a play

But even when this nightmare ends
Do not ever again ignore
The artist in your being
The fire in your very wire
The heaven in your hell

Empty Set

Tears falling into ten oceans of nine
Blood flowing onto cement of stone
Sweat pouring down forehead low
Not allowing me to be me
Building no team of family

Laugh if you will
Guffaw if you must
But my life is unjust

Mocking me when one plus one equals three

Slapping me when what they think I
Should be is not what I am

When what they understand is less
Than what I comprehend

What I imagine is bigger than what
They reason

What I know is more than what
They can ever realize

Imposing their will on those
Who think differently

By filling craters with dust
Numbers with rust

This empty set of moss and loss
Floss and toss

They are the rain
I the meadow

I am the ground
They the spit

After All

The end comes before the beginning
Time spent suffering is wasted
Death always comes ahead of life
Intelligence is overrated

Reason ranks behind imagination
How I think is how I exist

Why I create
Is why I live

Christmas is my Halloween
Satan not my Jesus

Altar not as important as the pew
Priest not as significant
As the church goers

After all, we succeed despite failing

Loving while hating
Laughing yet crying

Selling but buying
Creating and destroying

Sprinting while sitting
Speaking yet sleeping
Jumping but standing still

Making peace and war
Finding light and darkness

We try to die by living a lie

After all
Only fear does not run dry

Ink

Flowing
Boeing
Going

In fine lines and gay poses
Labored twists and careful turns

Skating tightly across page
Like skateboard cement
Roller skates rink

Forming letters and formulas
Syllables and norms

Poetry and fiction
Prose and lyrics
Notes and votes

Proudly I pack six writing instruments
Loudly I capture two more
From a store

Black, blue or red

Feeling paper with hand
Undulating sand

Filling papyrus with wrist
In early morning mist

I missed the list
With a closed fist

In the middle
A dangling cyst

Producing grist for
Readers to assist

Ink, oh, mighty ink
Do not blink
For you are exploding
In the sink

With your timely missing link
In this pink cauldron of
Wink and zinc

Pen, you stink

Barbara

(For Barbara Bagwell)

Coming around again
To the beauty in you

Angel stew
Angle in view

You are a poet
In soul and mind
Goal and time

The love
Inside and out

Giving way to
The substance within

Like a meteor
Your spirit soars

Like a comet
Style appears

Hitting the sky
A late missile

Singing very high
A fate epistle

Etching a Sketch

This is no painting or portrait
Still life or Salvador Dali number

It is the beginning of the beginning
A sketch before the real thing

An etching of the future
A sort of measurement of possibility

Transporting me away from the masks
Hand washing
Six foot social distancing

The two inches officials at
White House COVID press conferences
Stand away from each other

The sketching taking me to nirvana
My heaven
Our utopia

Away from hoarding in the supermarkets
Rudeness on highways and byways

And the indifferent difference on
Sidewalks and street corners

I sketch to learn more about
Myself and those around me

During these uncertain and confusing times
I etch to hang Covid-19 with its
Own tongue

Drown this pandemic in
Its own spit
Etching my sketch

Olive Blue

Hours of practice
Not being me

On this cobalt marble
Unique as Brie
Wearing cuffed wrists

In heavy mists glued to
Steel cages
Empty pages

Time does not change for me
Looking outside in
Like I was a sin

Negating myself to please those around me
Apologizing today
For tomorrow

Saying hello to stop from offering
Good-bye
Neon pink sky over heart felt sigh

Electric orange sun bending into metal gun
All I do is isolate and write
Like a Siamese cat without sight

Wondering how to keep my mind
From going insane

In puddles of death and
Fractured rain

Arithmetic another name for
Equations of a different frame

Often slowing the speed
To find the muse
Magenta fuse

Only to see it destroyed by
Bitter minds and ribald rhymes

It is time to find me
Among the steepest angle of debris

Motel Mate

Light washes over me at 6:43 a.m.
Like my mother's love
Father's paranoia
Sister's envy
Ex brother-in-law's soft hands and weak demands

The sun in its
Orange neon heat

The coronavirus kicker
COVID-19 licker
Pandemic fixer

Murdering eight strains of corona circling the globe
Strangling them in their sweat
Stomping them like an MMA bet

As in "The War of the Worlds"
Where the virus dies on its own
Heat is our best friend
Sunrays poisoning the virus into retreat
Dead on its feet

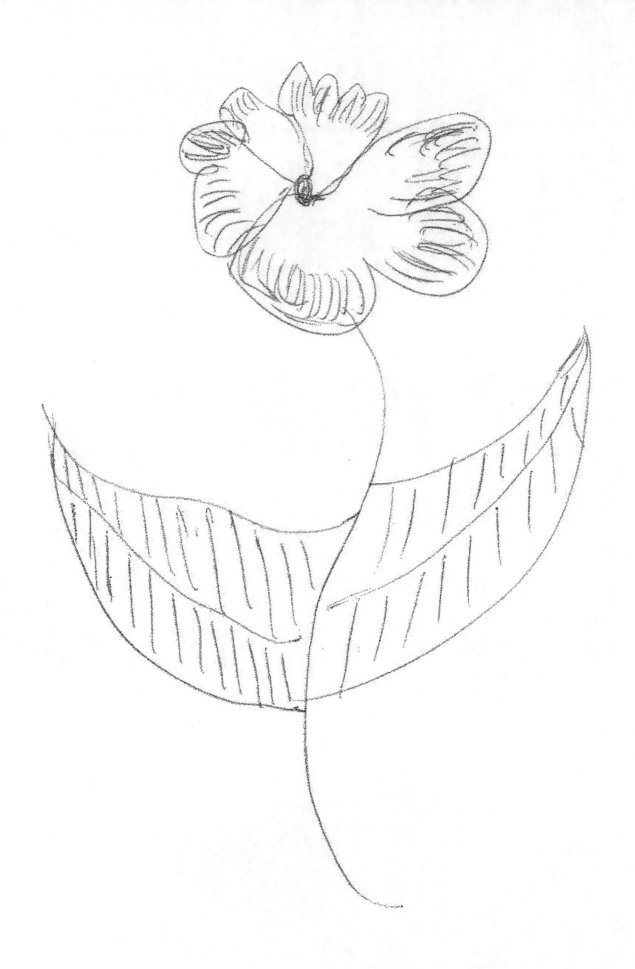

Sting Ring

In the sea of shattered dreams
I am confounded by current themes
Having nothing to do with the story's seams
Steam cleaning the smallest of
Paper reams

Owning blueberry pie sky
Like angels in July

Here in Hollywood only actors
Finding it sad
Poets shimmering in its radical fad

Motion pictures like fractured fixtures
Manufactured mixtures

Some last like water
Others slaughter time's only daughter

In the meadow of umbilical chords
Yours at least has no boards, Fords or
Bellowing hoards

It is safe in its nest
Like an owl its chest

The beginning of this end
Finding comfort in a rolling bend

Of green grass
Translucent fauna
Lush, golden blend

The Valley's Volatile Voice

Dips ramming ships
Guitars shredding doors
Suits bouncing on asphalt like so many boots

Sitting in my 2012 Barcelona red
Toyota Prius in the late afternoon sun

Cars going by like so many scars
Ventura Boulevard seems a dream
A Southern California fashion seam

San Fernando Valley donut cream
On this mid-Winter Wednesday
The boulevard has a mind of its own

Posing naked bone for bone
Stone for stone

Turn up the radio
The Beatles are on

Lips leading hips
People walking the cement sidewalk
In jeans and shorts
Greens and ice cream quarts

Time a history lesson
Meaning nothing
Signifying even less

Yellow electric
Neon orange

Side streets melting in pistachio
And cowboy blue

Garage signs and express car
Washes

I am alone again
Like hammer on head
Dinner in bed

At the Theatre Again

Tears rolling down crimson cheeks
Like streaming tributaries

Hands calm as jettisoned rattlesnakes

Just me and the actors
Seeing them
Hearing them
Smelling them
No screen between us
Speakers or 3-D glasses

Merely people talking to people
On that very special place called the stage

How lucky I am to live in a time when
Theatre is still important
Continues to matter

Where there is no barrier between
The actors and audience except
The one created by the playwright

Electricity in the air
Now in my front row chair

After all, where would we be without it?

Watching Spiderman again and again
On the back of some airplane seat

Soul filled with regret
Heart a second bet
This is humanity's chosen set

Women in A Flat

Monica, that final a
Dangling stray

Making its way to mischief and mayhem

All the females with names ending in a
You have changed me
Slayed me
Upheld me
Often killed me

Yet I love you all
For you are a forest of fury
Meadow of worry
Boulevard of judge and jury

Sylvia, Sabrina
Brenda, Petra
Dina, Jessica
Maruska, Blanka
Dana, Patricia

Hoist me on my front
Toss me into the mountain air

Let me know what it is to be a man
Understand me
Touch me
Love me

Please do not misunderstand me

For through you I see the sun
Gather the moon
Set the stars ablaze

Cut through you to get to me
Massage the a to clear the way

Girls in a minor
None finer

Tickle and Tattle

Watching too much television
Housewives of New Jersey and
Summer House on Bravo like a
Winter blouse

A wretched mouse
Making a big noise signifying nothing
Contributing not to our social and
Civil lot

Getting as far away from the tv
As my mangled legs will take me

Learning little but to find more
Of the middle

Alcohol and salad how absolutely invalid

I do not understand this generation
This variation

Social media and materialism
Trolls and ugly souls
Apps and shallow laps

Where is the spirituality?
The Maker?
The cross?
The big Oak with gray moss?
22 minutes of bloody floss

Bruised Like Bison

On the blue bus to Santa Monica, CA
They came at me in waves every morning
Like General Patton's tank brigade

Fingers, thumbs and hands
Men more interested in
What they could devour
Than what they could learn

What made their loins feel good
Than what made their souls soar

Fending them off day after day
With everything but clay

I was as vulnerable as a frightened child
Ready as a sprinter at the gun
Strong as Hercules on top of Mount Aetna

I judge them not
For fallible we all are
Until we heal the scar

Through the Plastic of Your Soul

The mannequin lips
Botox hips

Help me see the wonder of your flips
The ones that take your ideas and
Make them jello

The fiberglass heart that darts
Towards purgatory's mart

Leaving brothers and sisters behind
In decades of Winters frayed
Autumns dismayed

Throwing fuel on the blaze
Opening your legs to the haze
Knocking knees in this maze

Trembling wrists in this phase
Take those tender fists
And grow a spine

The one holding you together
Is a crime

Tortured Tributary

Building dreams from inglorious seams
Like sleeping in bed with the living dead

I only know of the heaven in your hell
The wine in the punch
Feeling anything is like a wall crumbling

Your fingers burning from cold water
Your brain billowing in the slaughter

Time is no friend
Roads bend

Sewing aspiration from
False perspiration

The meadow below pink with roses
Unholy poses

Erasing those bold directions
Like sex offenders without an erection

Galloping from person to person
Like ricocheting doll in hands too small

I do not understand your trembling voice
The trouble you make to
Avoid drowning in the lake

Rocks at the ready
Gate steady

Let sanity go
The child that said no
Reason for reason stow
Branded soul
Abandoned foal

Only you can stop a bleeding river
Without a goal

Broken Bank

If the days that pass
Are longer than the days that remain

If the love I take
Is equal to the love I make

If the closed door is
Thicker than the open one

If the sweat you break
Is greater than the perspiration you fake

Then the possibility you leak
Is weaker than the probability you seek

Then and only then, my son
Will you touch the moon

When the heaven you want
Is the nirvana you can't

When the angels floating
Are not the gargoyles voting

Then and but then will the sky open
And the children begin coping

The ground closing beneath the asphalt street
The very cement sidewalk seat

Then and only then, my brother
Will you banish the sun without a gun

Bain Drain

Days pass
Weeks amass

Still no peace
Inner tranquility

Down in the living room near the neon meadow
Sins are committed that last a lifetime
Injuries taken that never mend

Then there is you and me
Staking out common ground
The kind that leads to perfect sanity
In an insane universe

Hours go by
Still no sign of the heart that stopped
Afternoon topped

The man and his Celtic moon
The soul and its epic swoon

Please do not talk to me of depression or mental illness
But of a broken heart burning out
Like a matchstick in a lagoon

Of a fallen hero taken too soon
By a God dreaming in colors
We do not understand

Only to demand friendship and love
Like a rubber band

The former difficult to create
The latter too much of a stand

Both stolen by a Maker
An honest deal breaker

Lost to many
Two sides of a penny

Blazing like fire
Crushed by church spire

Eel to Steal

The end came without a beginning
Like a hole in the shield of gods

Soon rain will fall
Snow hail
Time wail

And I am here in Winter
Trembling in Bermuda shirt
Shivering in park where sex is free

I don't need a degree to succeed
But a brain on gain

The middle started yesterday
With no today

On instinct I run
Like flying nun

Life too long for contracts and yard sales
Existence fueled by rough rivers
Tough gales

The kind without broker or fire stoker
Perhaps there is no tomorrow

For our sorrow
Group marrow
Too narrow

Hiding behind porches and ovens
Only the dead beseech

Is it not fate
For seven to be eight
Death late?

An iron gate
Made of love and hate?

Hiding behind porches and ovens
Only the dead beseech

Black Ink

I do not want to write
Filling paper with ink
Papyrus with words

Why does my blood run hot with poetry?
My soul drowning in verse
Heart baking in written word

Being staked in art and flying bird
Language of another herd

Maybe my maybes are no maybes at all
Merely eagles soaring across frozen rivers
Cheetahs springing through wet fields

Time has no bottom
Existence no top

Alliteration dancing with metaphors
Subject mixing with syntax
Work wavering like rain

I am dark inside
Staining hide
Blocking ride
Knocking guide

Writing for sight
World finding light

Blaming Beelzebub

Flying to stand
Sitting to fall

We blame the devil
God's early foe
When we are at fault

And the stakes are low with blame, shame
And lack of real game

Wizards without wands
Emperors with no crowns
Prime Ministers planning coups
Presidents new political zoos

We are all comets, meteors and falling stars
Battling Beelzebub like moons to Mars

If I stay true with eyes tender and blue
It matters not how many opponents assemble
For I will always emerge victorious

With rod and staff at my side
Beelzebub is barbecued
Satan sautéed
The devil drugged

The never ending battle belonging to us
It is our fuss

Blaming Beelzebub for our sins
Castrating Satan for our deeds

We must start again with a new zen
One that spray paints its own turf
With original pen

Bending only to rattle red hen
Never breaking midnight wren

Ava

Ride that pole
That pole of vex

Into the soul
That soul of hex

Number 290 on Pornhub.com
I wonder where you rank
In all that dank

Or are you real at all
My brunette beauty?

At 18 you prove us all wrong
Long on show
But short on grow

Please my beautiful girl
Avert that gaze
To some other maze
Starting a new phase

Finding you all used up by the male race
Taking that
Sucking this
Oh, dear spirit where do you live?

Not making room for a take and give
Working for money not honey
Outlook less than sunny

Naked before us all
Camera in the stall

Smile my midnight-haired whistle
For you are thin as a thistle

Lying on that cold, wet table
Where only Jesus is able

Concrete Breakdown

Record stores empty as abandoned whores
Tent cities all over public land
Apartment buildings on Hollywood sand
Bungalows gone

Like history's pawn
Peacock song

Los Angeles my lady
Show biz Sadie
Always hazy
On the flip side of crazy

This concrete breakdown
Familiarity bred
Platinum path lost amid freeway rain
Asphalt pain

Nerves jangling
Brain wrangling

Lips removing
Hips not improving

Puddle without bottom
Muddle with problem
Huddle with too many helmets

Dead ocean drowning potion
All things too many
No rings less than a penny

My golden city on a hill
Taking too many pills

Rusting rotten
Dusting cotton
Busting motten

Into red
Losing its head
Time moving like God's bed

Black Turning Blue

In this incendiary Summer of storm and mourn
I lay fingers on chest
Feet on shore
Fists in air

And attack the back
The very flank
Where I am as vulnerable

As Sylvia Plath to husband Ted Hughes
And Macbeth his lady

I wear pain like a nickname
Love like new stain

Perhaps after I am through
The ambulance rose red and Redwood strong
Will save you from you

After all I have not done well reaching for your door bell
Your very eyes that open on my skull
My whitest of faces

I am turning black to blue
Learning not to pretend to love you

The valleys are mountains
Rain sunshine
Snow the most comfortable of breezes

Blowing blue to you
It is women who keep us true

Men are creatures of a different hue
Anti-virgins without a clue

Weeping Wall

Beneath the artificial lights
Pandemic heights
Transparent nights

I practice my rights
Which do not include fights
With the self-absorbed
And misled

Under the virus' cutting vine
I count till nine
To empty the line

Then I cry as if tears had no
Moratorium

Cheeks no clear sanitarium

Weeping bringing me back to me
The old and young
Skewed and true

Petrified and diseased
Abused and used

Like emptying my bowels
In a friend's backseat vowels

I take napkin to salt water
And wipe away the sun

Only then do I understand
God's plan on this Pepsi Cola
Can island of war and greed

Jealousy and need
Pestilence and feed
Love and lead
Dove and bead

Road to Death Valley

Through crushed roses
Shattered poses
Scattered noses
In the skeleton's skull
The truth emerges

Over dark meadows
Transparent shadows
I murder the only thing I know
Slowly molesting my garden of woe

Breakfast at midnight
Dinner for fools
There is an arrow meant for a mule

Cement and asphalt
Asphalt and cement
Streets stretching into beginning of end

Devil's disguise
Soul's lies

A wonderland of didactic wheels
Turning, turning towards
The steering gear

Where maybe just maybe
Silence is raped
Without a finger vaped

The human beings in the cage
Are all the rage

For power is the sage
Boulevard of dreams ripped apart
At the seams

Mutilated Metaphors

So what is this damaged dogma?
Staccato strategy
Wearing Zeus on head of
Depressed moose

The poetry mediocre
Rhyming local

The athletic metaphors
Back in the game
Like sullen linebackers

This duel literary battle
As good as forsaken cattle

Molested poems
Battered predicates
Golden afternoon to the ravaged rare

On this table of round
Lie bronze cantations
Processed as plantations

In a small hamlet where everyone cares
Ripping open the verse to the heart of the lair

Only then and there will existence glare
Time offer but a hair

For the rape of a metaphor on
The cusp of crime
Like a torn waif breathes
Joyous agony
Into that lifeless mime

Lucky Notebook

Pages blazing like wildfire
Animals charging like Indians downhill

Don Quixote in one corner
Don Adams in the other
Crows cawing
Butterflies gliding

This is my lucky notebook
Rusting and dusting
Fasting and blasting
Roasting and boasting

Thoughts just for me
Ideas owned by my soul
Poems, I promise, mainly poems

From embryo to flower
Seed to need
Literary greed indeed

Ink blossoming
Rink welcoming
Poems popping
Lips dropping

My book of note
Never not open for a good quote

Everything here open for debate
Except the love I have for my mate
Answering to another fate

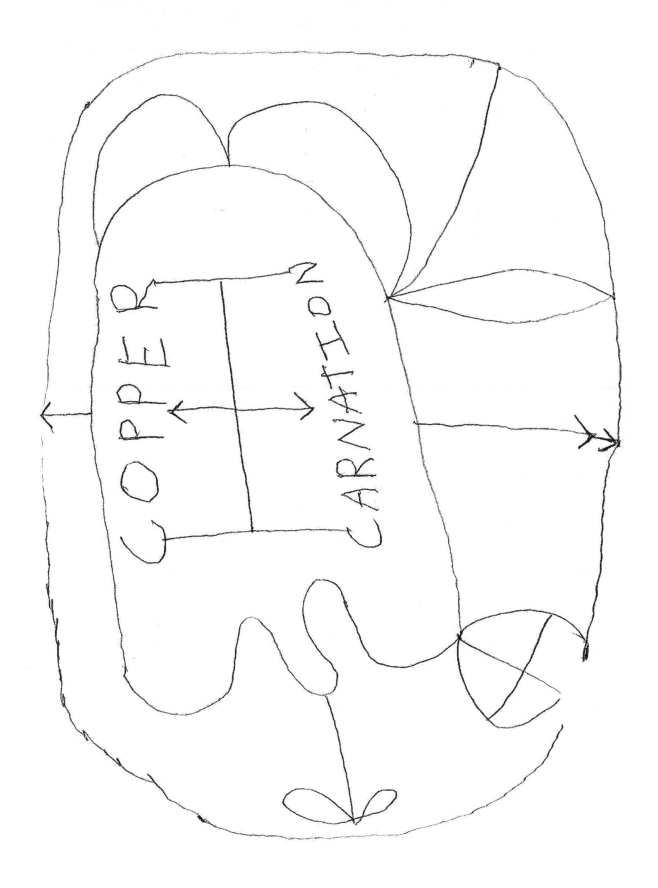

Box In The Jack Girl

I swear you are the most
Beautiful woman I have ever seen

While ordering Jumbo and
Double Jacks from your drive-thru
In Santa Clarita, CA
I fell in love with you at the window

You are what makes girls so mysterious
And fascinating

You are beyond explanation

You had me fixated from beginning
To end on your grace, courage and beauty

I do not know your name
And maybe it's better that way

Tugging and pulling at the memory of you
Like a boy his mother's skirt
Just won't do any longer

I want all of you or none of you
Like one of your large Oreo malts

Broken and Bruised

The bridge I jumped from yesterday
Is steeper today
The avenues I crossed never coming into play

Please tell me that I am not wrong
Never owning a bong

While children played in dusty stadiums
And waved dirty white flags

I am broken and bruised
Stepped on and confused

God cannot help me
Jesus does not save me

Please dearest my fate depends on you
Calling your name from the furthest lane
I wish to connect the dots between you and me

Marching with that invisible army
Breaking us down
Not even time the dancer can best our crown

Parking in high water like the devil's daughter
Did not stop me from leaving this slaughter
Nirvana can you tell me
Why I abuse such sharp fodder

At the Target in North Hollywood, CA Again

The red and white cave of capitalism
Plays host once more to this Czech lad
At the glass door begging for more

Slithering through the aisles
In a mini Handicapped Honda
With steel basket

I own the shop with
My Lymphedema hop

Half the people do not know
Why they are here

The other half
Want to be somewhere else

Everything inside this crimson cannery
Has a price
Even greed

Many buy just to buy
Others halfheartedly fill
The magenta shopping carts
Like divas at a high school prom

I purchase sportswear and CD's
As if they are extinct

And in this age of dinosaurs, dollars and dingoes
They probably are

Oh, sultan of sales
Restless and pale
I adore every square foot of your jail

Lymphedema Lost

When I ask
Because I ask
They shudder

For they melt like butter
Just about stutter

But I must decide
Playing by the rules or
Sitting on stools

This is my life
Naked strife

My path
Do the math

Illness which started below
Started above

Not with medication but predication
That I cannot take care of myself
Need help to steer the sea
Down on bended knee

The wraps are dirty
Legs not so sturdy

Confidence shaken
Like hurdy gurdy

Staring at swollen gams
Like growing yams

This must be my fault
I am to blame

Lymph nodes do not work
I am Captain Kirk
Not some Star Wars jerk

Spring Slasher

Coming with
Mid-afternoon showers

The slasher does anything
But scour

The petals separating from the very
Stem of the flowers

Swinging and stinging like Queen Bee
Dealing and stealing like bad hours

This slasher
Mad dasher

Has no conscience
Peppermint pink boots
Sun yellow apron

Smelling like carnations in the garden
Daisies in the field

His fame preceding him
Like Elvis Presley's pelvis

Every April sky bleeding blue
Clouds stealing anew
Time sitting on Everest like avalanche stew

Spring slasher playing by his own rules
Slaying all misbegotten fools

Yet there he is
Ketchup red
Pistachio green

Creating a
Brazen scene

On this alabaster island of frost and bite
Cold and night

Slasher cutting head off Winter
Harmonizing with Harold Pinter

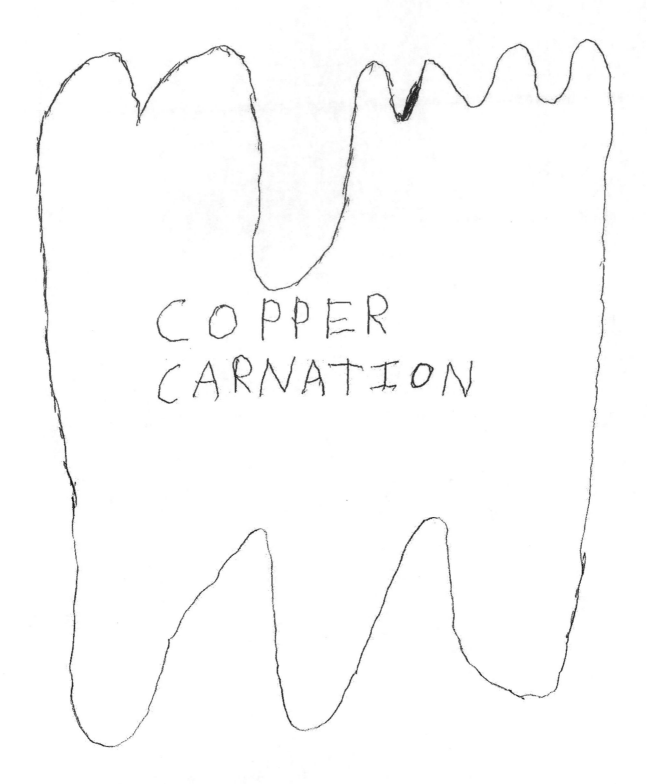

COPPER
CARNATION

Acknowledgements

COPPER CARNATION

1. Thrashed...Altadena Poetry Review (2019)

2. Patricia.....................................Spectrum Literary Journal (Pasadena, CA) (2020)

3. Pandemic Party....Covid-19 Anthology (Golden Foothills Press) (Altadena, CA) (2020)

4. Six Million Feet High......Shoah Remembrance Day (Poetry Super Highway) (2018)

5. Eyes Like Red Apples...Spectrum (2020)

6. Holy Hands...Covid-19 Anthology (GFP) (2020)

7. Etching a Sketch...Covid-19 Anthology (GFP) (2020)

8. Motel Mate...Covid-19 Anthology (GFP) (2020)

9. Weeping Wall...................Covid-19 Daily Website Poem (Highland Park Poetry)
(Chicago, IL) (2020)

10. The following twenty poems are featured in:

MENTAL MALL-Collection of Poetry
Four Feathers Press
(Pasadena, CA) (2020)
Sherbet Shark
Car Lights
Seeking Silver
Patricia on Key
Sunlight Through an Open Door

I Will Always Love You

Role

Stole

Mole

Hole

Laguna at Dusk

Writing on Her Mask

Fiance of Flowers

Thunderstorms like Long Deep Tunnels

Porcelain Plague

Thrashed

Mental Mall

Flowers With No Sages

Downtown

Patricia

Printed in the United States
by Baker & Taylor Publisher Services